CONTENTS

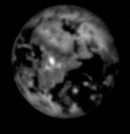

The Moon is located 384,400 kilometres from the Earth.

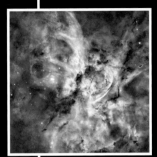

From a cloud of gas and dust...

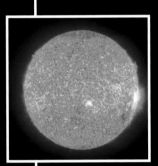

...our Sun was born. Rocks, metal and dust left over from the Sun's creation formed big rocky clumps...

...which became the planets of our solar system.

CHAPTER 1:
Our Amazing Planet

Our Earth is a ball of rock hurtling through space at around 108,000 kilometres per hour. Using satellites we can see the surface of our Earth from space. We see that its rocky surface is covered in vast blue stretches of water. Green plant life springs from the soil. And if we move closer, we can see towering rocky mountains and deep valleys.

BIRTH OF THE PLANET

Our planet's history began over 4.5 billion years ago. At that time scientists believe our solar system was just a huge cloud of dust and gas floating in space. Then the cloud began to collapse. The dust and gas spiralled inward.

Out of the dust and gas came a newly formed star – our Sun. Some of the dust particles that were left spinning around the Sun began to stick together. They formed large chunks of rocks. Some of these rocks were small enough to fit in your hand. Others were as large as mountains. These rocky chunks joined together and grew until they became rocky planets. One of these planets became Earth.

Planet Earth is about 150 million kilometres from the Sun. It is the third planet from the Sun in our solar system. This 'just right' position – neither too close nor too far – keeps the temperature of our planet moderate and stable. This is one factor that makes life possible on Earth.

White clouds float in the atmosphere (the layer of gases that covers our planet).

EARTH'S INGREDIENTS
Planet Earth is made up mostly of just eight elements. These include aluminium, calcium, iron, magnesium, oxygen, potassium, silicon, and sodium. Silicon and oxygen make up about 75 percent of Earth's rocks.

THE BLUE PLANET
Earth is a unique planet in our solar system. It is the only planet to have large quantities of liquid water on its surface. Without this water there would be no life on Earth.

AN EARTH YEAR
It takes the Earth 365 days, 6 hours, 9 minutes and 10 seconds to orbit the Sun. To complete one orbit, the Earth travels 941, 466, 240 kilometres.

BIRTH OF THE MOON
The Moon is Earth's only natural satellite. Scientists believe the Moon formed not too long after the Earth. One of the huge whirling masses of rock that were circling the Sun collided with Earth. Debris from the collision exploded into space and began circling Earth. There the debris formed the Moon in the same way that Earth was formed.

EARTH'S EARLY YEARS

As debris from space continued to pound the young planet Earth, the planet's surface heated and melted. Eventually, scientists believe, it was a huge sea of molten rock and metal. Each new bit of matter added to the mix and increased the planet's size.

At the same time, the molten rock released nitrogen, carbon dioxide and water vapour into the air. To this, the stream of debris added lots of dust. An atmosphere was forming around the planet, but it was a dark, dusty, and poisonous one!

Scientists are not sure when Earth's surface began to form a crust. But rocks about 3.8 billion years old have been found in Canada. Around this time, Earth's surface began to become solid.

This artwork shows the Earth as it may have looked during its molten phase. As planet Earth was forming, so were other planets. Eventually, about 4.3 billion years ago, our entire solar system took shape – eight planets orbiting the Sun.

EXTINCTION LEVEL EVENT

The Chicxulub Crater in Mexico has an impact crater of around 170 kilometres in diameter. Scientists believe the impact was caused by an asteroid or meteorite with a diameter of about 10 kilometres! The impact happened about 65 million years ago. The impact would have caused earthquakes, firestorms, tsunamis and catastrophic devastation on the Earth's surface. Some scientists believe this collision with space debris caused the extinction of the dinosaurs.

METEORITES

Today, bits of rock and metal are still shooting through space. Most of these pieces of space debris burn up when they hit the Earth's atmosphere. But sometimes they make it to the surface. When they do, we call them meteorites.

EVIDENCE OF PAST COLLISIONS

Earth's crust is marked by craters from prehistoric collisions between Earth and meteorites. Scientists estimate that over the past billion years there have been about 130,000 impacts that have produced craters with a diameter of one kilometre or larger.

The Meteor Crater in Arizona, USA, was formed between 20,000 and 50,000 years ago. The crater measures 1.2 kilometres in diameter. It was made by an asteroid measuring about 24 metres in diameter. It was the first crater on Earth to be identified as an impact crater.

SPACE DEBRIS

Leftover debris from the formation of our solar system is identified in the following ways:

METEORS/METEORITES

Meteors are chunks of rock and metal. As they enter Earth's atmosphere, they burn up and make a streak of light. When they do this we call them shooting stars. A meteor that hits Earth is known as a meteorite.

ASTEROIDS

Asteroids are jagged, rocky bodies. Most are found orbiting the Sun, between Mars and Jupiter in an area called the 'asteroid belt'. Some asteroids can be nearly 1,000 kilometres across.

COMETS

Comets are balls of frozen gas, dust and rock that orbit the Sun. As a comet gets close to the Sun, some of the ice on its surface evaporates. This releases dust to form a tail. A comet's dust tail can be 10 million kilometres long.

PLANET EARTH: INSIDE AND OUT

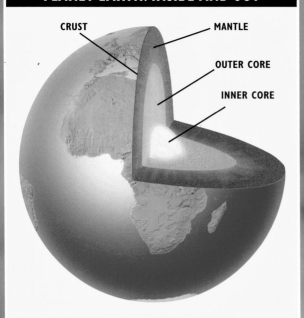

CRUST
MANTLE
OUTER CORE
INNER CORE

DIAMETER AT THE EQUATOR:
12,756 kilometres

DIAMETER AT THE POLES:
12,714 kilometres

CIRCUMFERENCE AT THE EQUATOR:
38,024 kilometres

WEIGHT (MASS) OF THE EARTH:
6.6 sextillion tonnes

DISTANCE FROM THE SUN:
150,000,000 kilometres

AVERAGE SURFACE TEMPERATURE:
15°C

THE PLANET AS WE KNOW IT

Earth's surfaces began to cool and form a crust.
But even then, the planet was molten inside.
Melted rock, called magma, churned and flowed,
and sometimes still burst onto the planet's surface.

All of this heat and movement released huge amounts
of water vapour into the young planet's atmosphere.
More water was brought to the planet by comets.

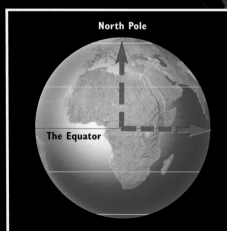

North Pole

The Equator

RADIUS OF THE SPHERE

Earth is not a perfect sphere. If it were, its
radius at the poles would be the same as
the radius at the Equator. Earth has a slight
bulge at the Equator. Therefore, at the
Equator, the planet's radius is slightly
greater than at the poles. There is a
difference of about 43 kilometres between
the two measurements.

All of this water together was then taken up into the atmosphere. There the water gathered only to rain back down onto the planet. Low spots in the Earth's surface filled with water, and oceans, lakes and rivers developed. Earth, as we know it, began to take shape.

Today, our active planet is still cooling. But between its birth and today, Earth's structure has divided into three distinct layers. We call the three layers the crust, the mantle, and the core.

Mount Chimborazo, in Ecuador, South America, sits on the Equator. The diameter of the Earth is greater at the Equator than at the poles. Therefore, the top of Mount Chimborazo is actually the furthest point from the centre of the Earth!

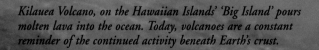

Kilauea Volcano, on the Hawaiian Islands' 'Big Island' pours molten lava into the ocean. Today, volcanoes are a constant reminder of the continued activity beneath Earth's crust.

OUR MOLTEN EARTH

SHAPING FROM WITHIN
Here, magma can be seen beneath the Earth's crust. Lava is magma that has reached Earth's surface. When lava pours from beneath Earth's crust it shapes the surface. This is one of the ways that scientists believe the planet developed.

ADDING TO THE LANDSCAPE
New lava flows out of and over previous flows. Just as with Earth's early crust, the lava cools and hardens at uneven speeds.

NEW TERRAIN
These plants are growing on a hillside formed from cooled lava and volcanic ash. After a volcano erupts, water, wind, heat and cold will break down the rocks and carry in sand and debris. Patches of soil will form where seeds can grow.

MOUNT EVEREST
Mount Everest is a peak in the Himalayan Mountains. It is the highest point on Earth. Mount Everest is located between Nepal and Tibet in Asia. It stands 8,850 metres tall.

THE DEAD SEA
The lowest point on Earth not covered by water or ice is along the shore of the Dead Sea. This salty inland sea borders Israel and Jordan. The shore is 400 metres below sea level.

CHALLENGER DEEP
If we include places on the Earth's crust that are under the ocean, then the Challenger Deep is the lowest point below sea level. This section of the Marianas Ocean Trench is in the northwest Pacific Ocean. Challenger Deep is 10,924 metres deep.

CHAPTER 2:
Earth's Layers

Earth's crust is the most visible part of the planet and the part we know best. The soaring mountains, deep valleys, and seemingly bottomless ocean trenches, make the Earth's crust seem 'rock solid' and almost indestructible. In reality, the crust is the thinnest and most fragile of Earth's layers. If you think of the Earth as an apple, then the crust is like the apple's skin!

EARTH'S BRITTLE CRUST

The Earth's landscape is quite different from place to place. This means the thickness of the crust is also different. It is thicker where there are high mountains, and thinner in deep trenches. Beneath the oceans the crust is generally about 7 kilometres thick. Where there are landmasses, the crust is an average depth of about 40 kilometres. Because the planet is covered by so much water, 70 percent of the Earth's crust is under oceans.

Uluru is a rocky outcrop in Uluru–Kata Tjuta National Park in central Australia. It stands 348 metres high. Scientists believe Uluru is the remains of an earlier mountain range. It is a good example of the differences in the Earth's crust.

The Grand Canyon, in Arizona, USA, allows us to see deep into the Earth's layered crust. The canyon is 446 kilometres long and about 1,829 metres deep at its lowest point.

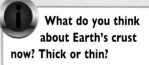

THE MANTLE

The mantle is the layer beneath the crust. It is the thickest of Earth's layers with an average depth of 2,900 kilometres. It is thought to be made mainly of silicon and oxygen.

UPPER MANTLE

The uppermost layer of the mantle is rigid like the Earth's crust. Below this is the thin asthenosphere layer. At this sub-layer, it starts to get very hot. Temperatures may reach 870ºC – hot enough to melt rocks!

Scientists believe that the asthenosphere is generally semi-solid. But, under heat and pressure, it can become soft enough to flow – slowly. Then it may be more like honey or melted tar.

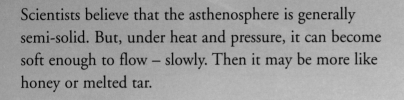

HOT SPOTS

A hot spot is an especially hot upper mantle area. Hot spots form when magma from the Earth's mantle rises to the surface. People in Iceland enjoy the benefits of living on a hot spot. Boiling magma close to the surface naturally heats lakes and pools. People can swim outdoors even in winter!

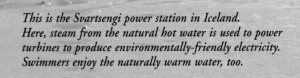

This is the Svartsengi power station in Iceland. Here, steam from the natural hot water is used to power turbines to produce environmentally-friendly electricity. Swimmers enjoy the naturally warm water, too.

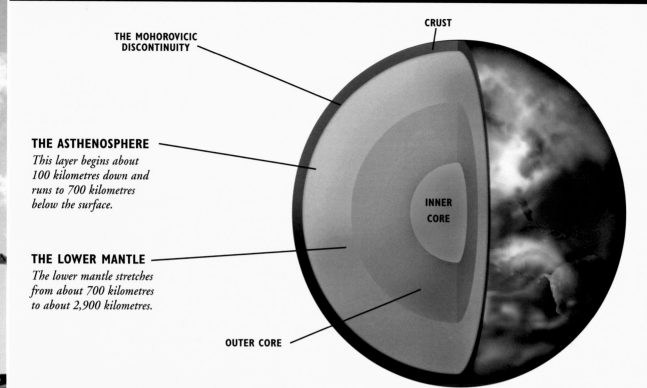

THE MOHOROVICIC DISCONTINUITY

CRUST

THE ASTHENOSPHERE
This layer begins about 100 kilometres down and runs to 700 kilometres below the surface.

INNER CORE

THE LOWER MANTLE
The lower mantle stretches from about 700 kilometres to about 2,900 kilometres.

OUTER CORE

THE MOHOROVICIC DISCONTINUITY

Croatian scientist Andrija Mohorovicic (1857–1936) studied earthquakes. He was interested in seismic waves – the motion caused by an earthquake. Mohorovicic studied the way the waves moved through the Earth. He was certain that a boundary existed about 35 kilometres below the Earth's surface. He was right. This boundary marks the end of the crust and the beginning of the mantle. It is known as the Mohorovicic Discontinuity.

LOWER MANTLE

The lower mantle is made mostly of silicate rocks (rocks composed of silica, oxygen and metals). There is also a lot of iron and magnesium. Moving toward the core, both pressure and heat increase. At the edge of the core, temperatures may reach 2,200°C.

At Yellowstone National Park in Wyoming, USA, the energy from a hot spot is believed to feed the park's many hot springs and pools. Old Faithful, one of the parks geysers, shoots about 31,800 litres of boiling water into the air every 76 minutes.

JOURNEY TO THE CENTRE OF THE EARTH

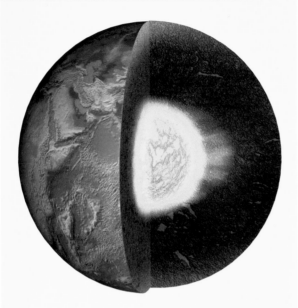

Scientists believe that at Earth's outer core the average temperature is about 2,200°C.

At the inner core temperatures may be as high as 5,000°C. That is just slightly less than the temperature on the surface of the Sun.

THE EARTH'S CORE

Earth's core is the layer that scientists know the least about. They believe it is made up of two layers – an outer, molten liquid layer and a solid inner layer.

The Earth's outer core is made mainly of molten iron and nickel. It is 2,200 kilometres thick.

Earth's inner core is thought to be made of metals such as iron and nickel, too. Because the materials are under great pressure at this depth, the core stays solid.

A blacksmith heats metal to make a horseshoe. The red-hot metal looks like lava and becomes soft. It behaves just like the metals of the Earth's outer core.

EARTH'S CORE AND ITS MAGNETIC FIELD

Earth's outer core is molten metal. As this mass moves, it spins the solid inner core of the planet. Scientists believe this motion, along with the core's heat, creates an electric current. That current creates a magnetic field around the planet. Earth behaves like a giant magnet.

The magnetic field that surrounds Earth is called the magnetosphere. It is a powerful force. It is the force that makes a compass point north.

This is a meteorite from Canyon Diablo in Arizona, USA. The meteorite is made of iron and nickel – the same ingredients as the Earth's core.

OUR PROTECTIVE SHIELD

The magnetosphere, Earth's magnetic field, has several important jobs. Among them is to act as a protective layer for the planet. This layer keeps out harmful materials from space, including solar wind. Solar wind is a flow of particles from the Sun. Like magnets, these particles have a charge. If these particles reached Earth, they could be destructive. Thanks to the magnetosphere, that does not happen often. This artwork shows the magnetosphere (blue) forcing the particles (orange) out and around the planet.

Sun

Earth

MAKE A TREASURE MAP

> **The compass is an old tool. Compasses were used by sailors and travellers to check the direction they were travelling in.**

Follow these simple steps to use a compass to create a treasure map for your friends to follow.

1) Stand with the compass in your hand. You should hold it as level as you can. Turn the bezel (the outside ring of the compass) so that north or zero lines up with the north-pointing arrow.

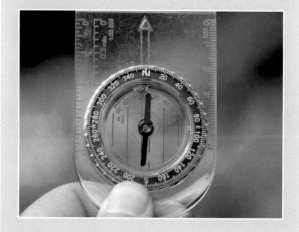

2) Pick a point a short distance away. Turn your body towards that point looking at it over the compass bezel. The direction indicated on the bezel (for example, east) is the direction that you will be walking in to get to that point.

3) Mark the place you are starting from then walk the distance to your destination, noting the number of steps you take. Record the direction and the number of steps from your starting point (for example, 40 steps east). Now repeat step 3 until you have created a route (for example east, 40 steps. North, 10 steps. West, 5 steps. South, 12 steps.)

4) Place something to mark the spot of your final destination – your treasure spot. Record all of your directions, along with the number of steps to be taken from one point to the next, on a map.

5) Ask a friend to follow your 'treasure map', using the compass.

CHAPTER 3: Our Restless Earth

Look at a map of the world. Do you think it's possible that if there was no ocean between the continents the landmasses might fit together? For example, would the west of Africa fit around the north of South America?

PANGAEA

In the late 1800s, and early 1900s, scientists began to study this idea. They investigated the idea that the Earth's continents were once a single huge piece of land. In 1912, German scientist Alfred Wegener (1880–1930) named this giant landmass 'Pangaea'.

EARTH'S JIGSAW

PANGAEA

The idea of continental drift suggests that about 250 million years ago, all of Earth's landforms were one continent. Scientists called this continent Pangaea. The name means 'all lands.'

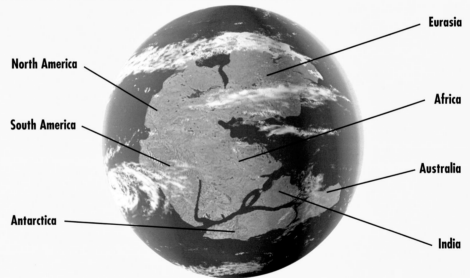

North America
South America
Antarctica
Eurasia
Africa
Australia
India

GONDWANALAND AND LAURASIA

By about 200 million years ago, Pangaea had split into two smaller masses. Gondwanaland included land that would become the southern hemisphere. Laurasia included land that would become most of the northern hemisphere.

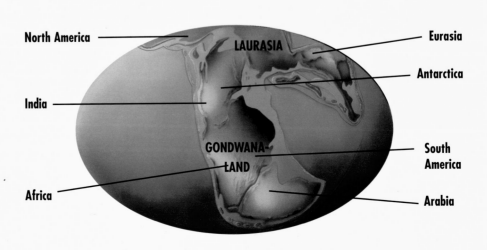

North America
India
Africa
LAURASIA
GONDWANA-LAND
Eurasia
Antarctica
South America
Arabia

CONTINENTAL DRIFT

In time, Pangaea split apart, and separate landmasses formed. These landmasses eventually became the continents we know today. This theory is now known as continental drift. Over millions of years the continents have drifted to their current positions. And they are still moving!

Scientists have gathered evidence to support this theory. They have discovered similar fossils on landmasses now separated by oceans. They have evidence of glaciers in places where today's climate does not suggest the presence of ice. They are able to show that the continents appear to 'fit together'.

CONTINENTAL DRIFT: FOSSIL EVIDENCE

The theory of continental drift answered the question of how similar fossils ended up on separate continents. Fossils of a prehistoric reptile called Mesosaurus had been found in the southern ends of both South America and Africa. The idea that the continents were once joined would explain how this freshwater reptile could be found in these two distant locations

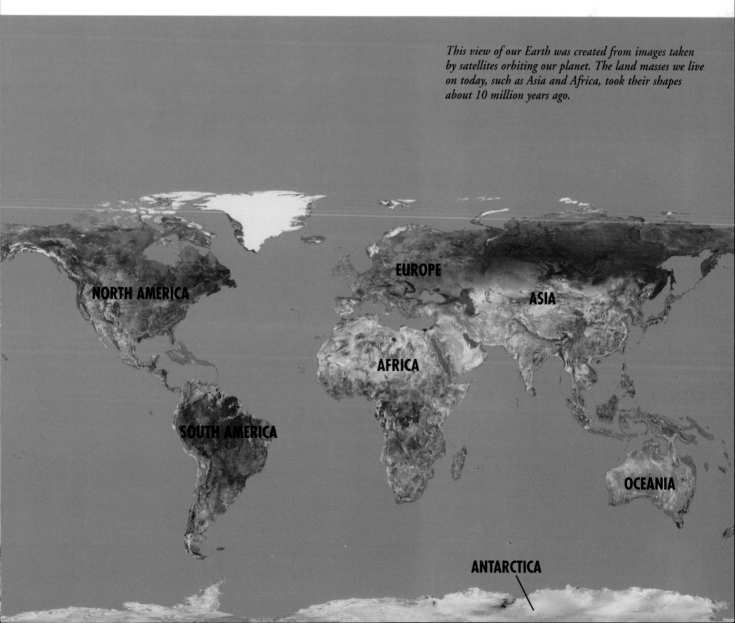

This view of our Earth was created from images taken by satellites orbiting our planet. The land masses we live on today, such as Asia and Africa, took their shapes about 10 million years ago.

NORTH AMERICA

EUROPE

ASIA

AFRICA

SOUTH AMERICA

OCEANIA

ANTARCTICA

EARTH'S TECTONIC PLATES

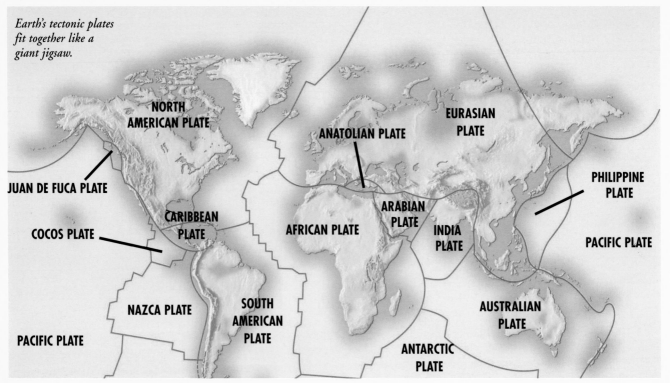

Earth's tectonic plates fit together like a giant jigsaw.

NORTH AMERICAN PLATE

EURASIAN PLATE

ANATOLIAN PLATE

PHILIPPINE PLATE

JUAN DE FUCA PLATE

ARABIAN PLATE

CARIBBEAN PLATE

COCOS PLATE

AFRICAN PLATE

INDIA PLATE

PACIFIC PLATE

NAZCA PLATE

SOUTH AMERICAN PLATE

AUSTRALIAN PLATE

PACIFIC PLATE

ANTARCTIC PLATE

Today, the continents are still moving. North America and Europe are slowly drifting apart at a rate of about 1.5 centimetres each year. The Atlantic and Indian Oceans get wider by a few centimetres each year, while the Pacific Ocean is very slowly shrinking.

CITIES ON THE MOVE

SAN ANDREAS FAULT

SAN FRANCISCO

LOS ANGELES

MOVEMENT OF THE NORTH AMERICAN PLATE

MOVEMENT OF THE PACIFIC PLATE

On the west coast of the USA, two tectonic plates meet along the San Andreas Fault. The two plates are moving past each other at an average rate of about 5 centimetres each year.

In around 11 million years the cities of San Francisco and Los Angeles could be next to each other!

PLATE TECTONICS

What the earlier scientists did not have was knowledge of plate tectonics. The Earth's crust and the rigid upper section of the mantle are known together as the lithosphere. The rigid lithosphere is broken into huge pieces, called tectonic plates.

The tectonic plates support the continents and oceans, but they are constantly moving. They float on the oozing, liquid mantle below – moving just a few centimetres each year.

Scientists now know that much of the change in Earth's crust is caused by the movement of the plates in the lithosphere.

FAULTS

As tectonic plates slowly move, they squeeze and stretch the rocks underground. An enormous pressure builds up. Sometimes the Earth's crust is put under such pressure that cracks appear. The places where the crust cracks are called faults.

The San Andreas fault is a 1,200 kilometre long fault that runs along the Pacific coast of the US.

EARTH'S CRACKED-UP CRUST

Materials needed
- Clear glass mixing bowl
- Clear honey
- Crackers

1) Pour a few centimetres of honey into the bowl.

2) Carefully drop the crackers onto the honey.

3) Imagine that the honey is the Earth's liquid mantle and the crackers are the tectonic plates. What do you observe happening?

> **Earth's temperature gets hotter toward the centre. The material also gets denser (thicker). This is what makes it possible for the mantle to support the crust even in its slightly melted state.**

4) Now push one cracker with your finger. How easily does it move across the surface of the honey? What do you observe when one cracker moves against another?

> **Moving one piece of cracker in the honey moves others – sometimes whether they touch or not. Earth's plates also affect one another as they move.**

INSIDE A VOLCANO

A volcano is a self-made mountain. Its hollow centre provides a pathway between the mantle and the surface.

The sides of the volcano grow steeper as the lava from each eruption builds up.

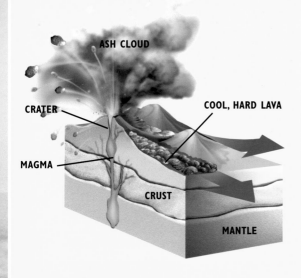

CHAPTER 4:
Changing Face Of Earth

Very active forces came together to create the Earth. Many of those forces continue to affect the planet today. Volcanic eruptions and earthquakes are natural events that affect and shape the planet's surface. They are also signs of activity within the planet's crust, mantle, and core.

VOLCANOES

Earth is dotted with volcanoes. Some are on the land. Some lie under the oceans. Many of Earth's volcanoes occur along the edges of the tectonic plates.

EARTH'S RING OF FIRE

Earth has over 500 active volcanoes. An 'active' volcano is one that has erupted in recorded history. This total does not include the volcanoes in the oceans. Counting them would increase the total by a lot. Many volcanoes are located along a path called the 'Ring of Fire.' This very active line of volcanoes is around the boundaries of the Pacific Plate. There is also a lot of earthquake activity here.

THE 'RING OF FIRE' IS SHOWN IN ORANGE.

Some volcanoes erupt along the ocean ridges as plates move apart. Others form where an ocean plate meets a continental plate. But not all. Some volcanoes simply rise up in the middle of a plate. These are created by hot spots.

Volcanoes are of special interest to scientists. A volcano's lava gives scientists a direct look at material from inside our planet. It also gives them evidence of processes taking place kilometres below the Earth's crust.

Sometimes magma breaks through the Earth's crust at a hot spot. When this happens under the ocean it can form islands. Every time the volcano erupts it grows bigger. One day the volcano erupts at the water's surface and forms a volcanic island. The Hawaiian Islands were formed this way.

IDENTIFYING LAVA

Lava takes different forms. It can be smooth, or crumbly, or even formed from big blocky chunks.

The form lava takes depends on:
• What it is made of
• How much gas is in it
• The temperature of the flow

PAHOEHOE FLOW
Lava that looks smooth and ropelike.

AA FLOW
Lava that is coarse and maybe sticky!

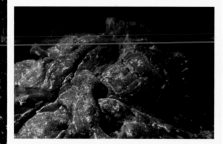

PILLOW FLOW
Lava that flows underwater.

During an earthquake, the Earth's crust can break along a fault. The rock on either side of the fault shifts, either sideways or up/down.

NORMAL FAULT
A normal fault occurs when plates diverge, or move away from each other.

REVERSE FAULT (DIP-SLIP)
A reverse fault occurs when plates converge or move toward one another.

SLIP FAULT (STRIKE-SLIP)
A slip fault occurs when plates move past one another in a horizontal, or side-by-side, path.

EARTHQUAKES

An earthquake begins with a build up of stress along a fault. The two sides of a fault are trying to slip past each other but they get stuck. The stress builds underground. The crust bends and flexes. Sometimes the bending and flexing does not relieve the tension. Suddenly, far underground rocks break and give way. Vibrations called seismic waves are sent out. They make the ground on the surface shake violently – an earthquake!

SEISMOGRAMS

A seismograph machine traces the vibrations caused by an earthquake onto paper. This record, called a seismogram, shows scientists the strength and duration of an earthquake.

TSUNAMIS

Earthquakes can occur at faults underwater too. When they do, this can cause a tsunami – a giant wave. The water absorbs the energy of the earthquake and waves ripple out from the earthquake's epicentre. The epicentre is the place on the Earth's surface directly above where the earthquake starts.

The waves can move out across the ocean as fast as 800 kilometres per hour. At this point, the waves may be small. But as they approach land they move into shallower waters. Then, they slow and start to build. As deadly tsunami waves hit a shore, they can be 30 metres tall!

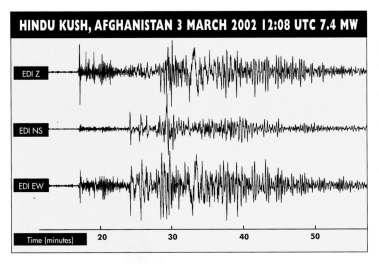

HINDU KUSH, AFGHANISTAN 3 MARCH 2002 12:08 UTC 7.4 MW

EDI Z

EDI NS

EDI EW

Time (minutes)   20   30   40   50

This is the seismogram of an earthquake in Afghanistan in 2002. The earthquake had a magnitude of 7.4. The bigger the earthquake, the bigger the peaks traced on the seismogram.

Rescue workers and survivors search in the rubble of a city following an earthquake in August 2007. The earthquake in Pisco, Peru had a magnitude of 8.

MEASURING EARTHQUAKES

The strength, or magnitude, of an earthquake is measured by scientists using a scale called the Moment Magnitude Scale. An earthquake of magnitude 'one' can only be detected by sensitive equipment. An earthquake with a magnitude of 8 is considered devastating! The world's largest earthquake was recorded in Chile on 22nd May, 1960. It had a magnitude of 9.5. Thousands of people were killed or injured, and two million people lost their homes.

MAGMA UNDER PRESSURE

Materials needed
• A tube of toothpaste   • A wooden skewer

Using a tube of toothpaste, explore how magma moves around inside the Earth's crust, mantle, and core.

1) Make sure the top to the toothpaste tube is screwed on tight.

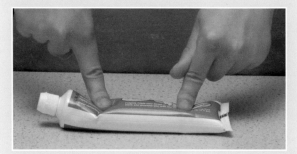

2) Use your thumbs and fingers to put pressure on the tube in different places. Observe how the contents of the tube move away from the pressure.

3) Now use the skewer to poke a small hole in the toothpaste tube. Squeeze again. The hole provides the trapped 'magma' with a way to release the pressure.

i Magma is often under pressure in the Earth from factors such as heat and layers of weight from above. When that happens, the molten rock will seek the nearest open space. The magma escapes and relieves the pressure.

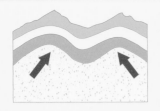

FOLD MOUNTAINS

Sometimes the plate movements can force rocks to push against each other, fold and rise up. Mountains are pushed up at upfolds and valleys form in downfolds.

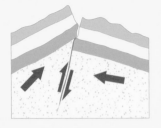

FAULT MOUNTAINS

Sometimes the Earth's surface cracks on a fault. Layers of rock on one side of the fault can be pushed up to form a mountain.

VOLCANIC MOUNTAINS

Some mountains are formed by volcanic activity. Volcanic mountains are formed from lava and rocks. After a volcanic eruption, the lava hardens and cools on the surface.

DOME MOUNTAINS

Sometimes heat from inside the mantle pushes the Earth's crust upward. This creates a bulge on the surface.

AN EVER-CHANGING PICTURE

The Earth's crust is constantly changing. Natural forces, such as heat, pressure, and movement from within the Earth cause these changes. On the surface, weather and erosion cause changes. But it is a long, slow process.

MOUNTAINS

Mountains are one of Earth's constantly changing features. Mountains are formed when the Earth's tectonic plates move. As the plates collide or move against each other, their boundaries deform. This causes huge, rocky landforms to appear on the Earth's surface – mountains. It can take thousands or millions of years for a mountain to form.

WEATHERING AND EROSION

The Earth's crust is also shaped by outside forces such as weathering and erosion. Weathering is the gradual break down of rock. Over time wind, water and other surface factors wear away the rock's surface until it crumbles. Then erosion takes over. Wind, water and even ice carries or blows the sediment away. This rock formation is the Three Gossips in Arches Park, Utah, USA. It shows the results of weathering and erosion over time.

The Andes are the world's longest chain of mountains. They were formed around 70 million years ago when the Nazca plate collided with the South American plate.

WATER AT WORK

Water is another factor in the constant change of Earth's surface. Rivers make huge changes to the landscape. As a river runs its course it can carve a deep valley into the Earth's crust. It can also carry sediment from one place and deposit it in another. The ocean changes the edges of the Earth's landmasses. It crashes into the shore and creates craggy cliffs.

The Gorges du Verdon is in France. This deep valley is being formed as the flowing Verdon River cuts its path. Notice the valley's V shape. A V-shaped valley is a sign of a young stream.

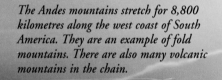

The Andes mountains stretch for 8,800 kilometres along the west coast of South America. They are an example of fold mountains. There are also many volcanic mountains in the chain.

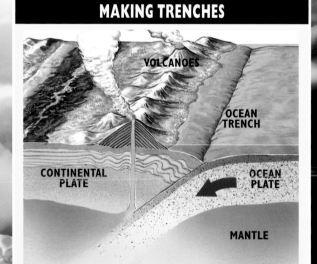

MAKING TRENCHES

VOLCANOES

OCEAN TRENCH

CONTINENTAL PLATE

OCEAN PLATE

MANTLE

Sometimes the Earth's plates move toward one another, forcing one under the other. This is called subduction. In the ocean, this can result in deep trenches.

Marble is a metamorphic rock. It is formed when limestone comes under great heat and pressure. Its colours and grain have made it a popular material. In ancient times it was used for carving statues. Today, your kitchen surfaces might be marble.

These layered sandstone formations in Antelope Canyon, Arizona, USA, have been formed by erosion from powerful, rushing flood waters.

CHAPTER 5:
Earth's Building Materials

The crust of our planet is made of rock. The tectonic plates move that rock. They crunch and fold it. They force rock from deep underground to the surface. Volcanoes heat up underground rocks and spew them out onto the surface. Rocks are constantly on the move and changing.

TYPES OF ROCK

The rocks of Earth's crust are made mainly from eight elements. But the way these elements combine creates many, many different kinds of rock. Scientists separate Earth's rocks into three groups.

Igneous rocks are formed from molten magma that has cooled and become solid.

SOIL - THE BASIS FOR LIFE

Soil is everywhere. Because it is everywhere, we sometimes forget how important it is. Without soil, plants couldn't grow. Plants are needed to produce the oxygen that humans and animals breathe. They are also a vital part of all land-based food chains.

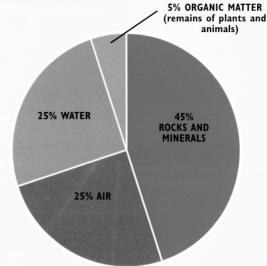

5% ORGANIC MATTER (remains of plants and animals)

25% WATER

45% ROCKS AND MINERALS

25% AIR

This chart shows the basic composition of soil everywhere.

Soil is created by weathering. Fine grains of rock and minerals combine with air, water, and organic materials. Soil differs from place to place throughout the world. But its basic ingredients remain the same.

THE ROCK CYCLE

The rock cycle is a constant process of change.
The rock cycle changes rocks from one type into another.
It is happening around us and under our feet all the time!

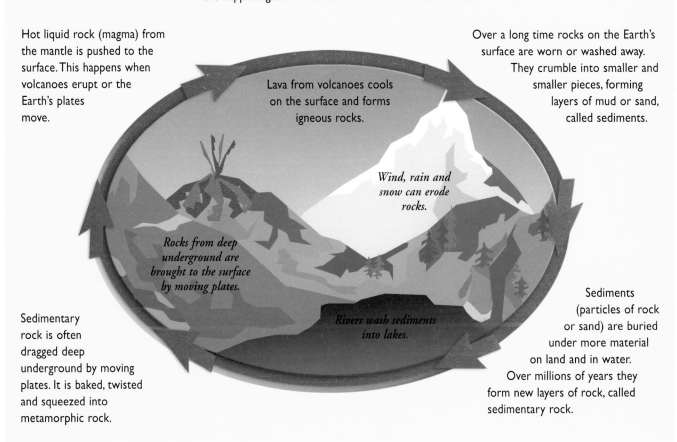

Hot liquid rock (magma) from the mantle is pushed to the surface. This happens when volcanoes erupt or the Earth's plates move.

Lava from volcanoes cools on the surface and forms igneous rocks.

Over a long time rocks on the Earth's surface are worn or washed away. They crumble into smaller and smaller pieces, forming layers of mud or sand, called sediments.

Wind, rain and snow can erode rocks.

Rocks from deep underground are brought to the surface by moving plates.

Rivers wash sediments into lakes.

Sediments (particles of rock or sand) are buried under more material on land and in water. Over millions of years they form new layers of rock, called sedimentary rock.

Sedimentary rock is often dragged deep underground by moving plates. It is baked, twisted and squeezed into metamorphic rock.

Metamorphic rocks form deep underground. Heat, pressure, and magma change these rocks. The original rock may take on a whole new makeup.

Sedimentary rocks are formed from layers of sediment (tiny, tiny grains of rock). These rocks can form on land or in water. They form wherever sediment is deposited. Over many years, the sediments are crushed until they join together and form rocks.

This granite mountain shows signs of another changing process called exfoliation. This is the process by which whole sheets of rock break off. The rock is then broken up into sediments. The waterfalls and streams in the mountains carry the sediment away.

STILL SEARCHING FOR ANSWERS

Technology in science is quickly improving our study of Earth's crust and core. Every day, it seems, we improve our ability to investigate our world. After an earthquake, for example, the Internet now offers information on the event for scientists worldwide. The location of the earthquake's epicentre, its magnitude, and its length and depth along a fault line are readily available.

Today, sharing information is important to scientists. A recent project in California, USA, is a good example. Scientists placed 250 global positioning system (GPS) instruments along the San Andreas fault. These instruments sense and record even small changes in the crust along this active fault. This project will soon become part of a bigger project run by a group of scientists known as EarthScope. These scientists come from many scientific backgrounds. They watch the entire North American continent.

SCIENTIFIC FORECASTING

It used to be that we wanted to find out if a volcano was going to erupt or if an earthquake might occur. Scientists now want to be able to tell when. They want to be able to forecast.

SCIENTIFIC FORECASTING

When a volcano erupts, scientists want to know who or what might be in its path? How much warning do people need to get out of the way? With the help of computer software, scientists are able to look at a volcano's pattern of eruptions, its shape, changes in that shape, and other details. This information is then used to forecast the next eruption – often accurately. The International Volcano Research Center in Arizona, USA, created such a program. It has been in use since 1988 and has been accurate in over 90 percent of its forecasts.

Learning anything about Earth is a matter of building upon ideas – yours, a fellow scientist's, history's. Who knows from where the next 'big idea' will come?

SEEING EARTH AS A SYSTEM

Very few events take place on Earth without affecting life around it. An earthquake causes a tsunami that crushes a coastline. A plate collides with another and folds into a mountain. A volcano erupts and causes a deadly mudflow.

Scientists have begun to look at Earth as a single system. They see everything as connected.

NASA in the USA has a program to look at this. It is called Earth Science Program. It overlaps different sciences to study the land, water, and air.

The program has three parts:
1) Satellites to watch the planet and collect information.
2) A system to review the information.
3) A team of scientists to study the information.

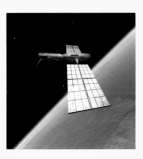

SG-3

The former USSR is among the countries that have attempted deep drilling projects. The Soviets' goal was to investigate the Earth's crust through deep drilling. They began drilling on 24th May, 1970, at the Kola Peninsula in the Arctic. They drilled for 24 years and dug a hole 12 kilometres deep. The Soviets did not get through the crust as they had hoped. But they did get rocks from a deeper part of the crust than anyone before had. Geologists had theories of what rocks at this depth would be like. Now they were able to compare actual rocks with their theories. The hole, named SG-3, is still the deepest hole ever made by humans.

Kola Peninsula

URAL MOUNTAINS

UK

EUROPE

ALPS

GLOSSARY

asthenosphere The thin, pliable layer of Earth's upper mantle on which the rigid crust can move.

atmosphere The thick layer of air that surrounds the Earth. The gases that make up Earth's atmosphere include nitrogen (78%) and oxygen (21%). There is also water, and small quantities of other gases such as argon, greenhouse gases and carbon dioxide.

atom All materials and subtances are made up of atoms. They are the smallest possible unit of an element that still behaves like that element.

core The core is the centre layer of the Earth's three layers. It is made up on an inner and an outer core. The Earth's core is about 3,400 kilometres thick.

crust The outer layer of the Earth. The crust is about 40 kilometres thick beneath the continental landmasses and 7 kilometres thick beneath the oceans.

diameter The distance measured by a straight line through the centre of a circle or sphere.

earthquake A violent shaking of the ground. It is caused by rocks deep underground cracking and breaking when they are put under stress due to movements of the Earth's tectonic plates.

elements Substances made up of a single type of atom. Elements can't be broken into simpler components by chemical processes. There are 92 naturally occurring elements, such as Hydrogen (H), Iron (Fe) and Silicon (Si). Some elements are liquid, some are gases, and some are solids.

erosion To carry away material by movement of wind, water or ice.

faults Cracks in the Earth's crust. The movement of the Earth's tectonic plates causes rocks to move and stretch until the pressure becomes so great that they crack.

fossils The remains of a once living thing, such as an animal or plant, preserved in rock.

glacier A huge, slow-moving river of ice (usually around 30 metres thick). The glacier moves slowly down a slope or valley. Some glaciers move only a few centimetres a year. Others travel up to one metre a day.

global warming A gradual warming of the Earth's atmosphere. Most scientists believe that this is caused by humans burning fossils fuels, such as oil and coal. The burning of these fuels gives off greenhouse gases that are trapping too much of the Sun's heat in the Earth's atmosphere.

Gondwanaland One of two landmasses thought to have formed when Pangaea broke apart some 200 million years ago. It is made up of land that now forms the continents of Africa, Antarctica, Australia, Asia, and South America.

greenhouse gases Gases such as carbon dioxide, methane and nitrous oxide. These gases trap heat from the Sun in the Earth's atmosphere – a lot like the glass roof of a greenhouse traps the Sun's heat.

igneous rock Rocks formed from magma that has reached the Earth's surface and cooled. To remember that igneous rocks are caused by great heat and fire, think of the word 'ignite'.

landform A feature on Earth's surface such as a mountain.

Laurasia One of two landmasses formed by the breakup of Pangaea some 200 million years ago. Laurasia was made up of land that now forms Europe, North America, and parts of Asia.

lava Molten material made of rock, gas and other debris that comes from an erupting volcano. Before it reaches the surface, this material is known as magma.

lithosphere The hard outer layer of the Earth formed from the crust and the uppermost part of the mantle. On average, the lithosphere is about 100 kilometres deep. The word lithosphere comes from the Greek word 'lithos', which means 'stone'.

magma The fiery, flowing mix of rock found in Earth's mantle and outer core. The heat and pressure inside the Earth keeps the material in this semifluid state. When magma manages to escape to the surface of the planet, it is called lava.

mantle The Earth's middle layer. The mantle has an average thickness of 2,900 kilometres.

metamorphic rock Rock that has been transformed into a different type of rock. Most metamorphic rock forms because of great heat and pressure deep within the Earth. To remember this process think of the word 'morph', which means 'to change'.

Moment Magnitude Scale A system used by scientists to measure the strength and size of an earthquake.

Orbit When one object, such as a planet, makes a complete circuit around another object, such as the Sun, usually on a circular or oval path. This movement is continuous.

Pangaea The name given to the large land mass that existed about 250 million years ago. Pangaea was made up of all the land masses that form the individual continents we live on today. The existence of Pangaea is part of the theory of continental drift.

planet Any large body in space that revolves around as star as part of a solar system. Earth's solar system includes eight major planets: Mercury, Venus, Earth, Mars, Jupiter, Saturn, Uranus, Neptune.

plate tectonics The study of the movements of the Earth's tectonic plates.

radius The length of a straight line from the edge of a circle or sphere to its centre.

satellite A body that revolves around another larger body in space. The Moon is Earth's only natural satellite.

sedimentary rock A rock formed from layers of sediment. Over many years, pressure from the layers above combined with heat packs the sediment together until they form new rock.

solar system A group of planets orbiting a star, such as our Sun.

tectonic plates The giant jigsaw-like pieces of the Earth's crust. The plates float on the Earth's mantle and are constantly moving at a very slow rate.

tsunami A Japanese word for the huge and damaging ocean waves caused by earthquake vibrations under the ocean.

volcano A hole in the Earth's crust through which gas, ash, and magma escape from the mantle. Volcanic eruptions cause a mountain to form made from lava that has cooled and hardened.

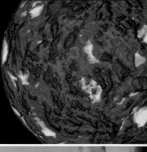